D1809977

TIME TRAVELLERS
at the bottom of the garden

to Dr Wynne - Jones

with grateful thanks for all your
care and patience for my
late wife, Rakıyah .

from Michael Beswick

For Rakiyah,
In memory of a dedicated gardener,
her gardening and her gardens.

First published in Great Britain in 2010 by
Michael Beswick,
Box 244, 111 Piccadilly, Manchester M1 2HX.
thebeswicks93 @ btinternet.com

Copyright © Michael Beswick

No part of this publication may be reproduced in any material form,
whether by photocopying or storing in any medium by electronic
means, whether or not transiently or incidentally to some other use
for this publication without prior written consent of the copyright
owner, except in accordance with the provisions of the Copyright,
Designs and Patents Act 1988, or under the terms of the licence
issued by the Copyright Licensing Agency Limited of 33-4
Alfred Place, London WC1.

British Library Cataloguing in Publication Data
A catalogue record for this book is available from the British Library.

ISBN 978-1-907373-10-7

TIME TRAVELLERS
at the bottom of
the garden

A life in gardening by Rakiyah Beswick
with drawings by Michael Beswick

Foreword

Rakiyah Khan arrived in Liverpool in 1959 from Alexander Village, Ruimveldt, British Guiana, and met Michael Beswick, an architectural student at the University in 1960. They married, had three children, moved from Liverpool to Northampton, Karachi, Kettering, Bedford and finally to Marple. Rakiyah's tropical background influenced the way in which she approached gardening in England, taking her inspiration from her grandmother's self-sufficiency in British Guiana. Added to this was a growing interest in British native plants gathered from hedgerows, woods and parks wherever they lived. The lessons learned from plant communities and the relationships within plant families informed the selection of plants in her gardens, making it possible to grow hardy species which could survive in the British climate whereas their tropical cousins perished, even indoors. She became fascinated by the medieval principles of growing plants which are useful, fragrant or beautiful and applied these to give a purpose to gardening which generated so many other activities. Rakiyah's evangelistic zeal to communicate her discoveries to as many people as possible was expressed in an exhibition on her "Passion for Plants" at Bedford Library, and imparted in talks to about thirty different groups around Bedfordshire. A slot on "Gardeners World" and radio interviews followed.

Since his retirement from Local Government in 1991, Michael devoted ten years to botanical drawing in an attempt to keep pace with Rakiyah's appetite for new plants with different uses and fascinating stories. Many of his drawings were exhibited at Royal Horticultural Society shows in London and Rakiyah wrote all the captions describing the essential details of her plants. But they believed, like H E Bates, that the garden is a living entity, so the florilegium reflects this and, like the garden, could never be finished. Failing health meant that they both had to reinvent the way they did their gardening, so many plants finished up in pots for ease of maintenance on the kitchen table. They eventually moved to a house with a small patio which became home to their pots.

Rakiyah died in 2010, still dreaming of acquiring another garden and with next year's seed catalogues around her to add more treasures to her box of seeds, her box of hopes.

This book brings together all the written material she put together for exhibitions, her thoughts set out in leaflets given away at her talks, and transcripts of television and radio interviews. These have been edited by Michael who added links from his own memories of a lifetime of exchanges on gardening subjects with his wife of almost 48 years.

The Roots

The miniature cultivar Punica granatum 'Scarlet Devil' is the closest I came to growing my own pomegranates in a pot.

The first seeds of my journey into gardening were sown in British Guiana when I was a teenager in the 1950s. I grew up with plants all around me and, like all children in the community, I knew exactly where to find a flower from which you could suck the honey or a shrub which bore a delicious berry. My father would bring home jasmine flowers tucked into his astrakhan cap, just for me to enjoy their perfume as I did my homework. My brother often went on hunting and fishing expeditions up "the Backs", and he would always bring back a flower bud of the *Victoria regia* lily for which he had waded deep into streams with a cutlass and a thick jute bag to protect him from its wicked spines. I would wait all night for it to open.

All these things were an essential part of my childhood, as was a visit to my grandmother who lived in the countryside on the other side of the Demerara River. Until the day she died at over 90 years old, she was self-sufficient in her Paradise garden - or so it seemed to me, having travelled a world away from her idyllic existence. Memories of the oleander tree by her steps flooded me with nostalgia.

"How far from me that first kiss by the oleander tree,
How far from me those warm hands embracing me."

Things we thought of in England as exotics were everyday fruits and vegetables in British Guiana: mangoes, papayas, ginnips, okras, aubergines and background supply of herbs and spices were taken for granted. The image of waxen flowers of pomegranates danced in my head like scarlet candles hedging the garden and its luscious fruits hanging from the branches like the decorations of Solomon's temple. They hung over a flowing stream and you would risk your life to pick them. Her coconut palms gave her not only the coconut for cooking and the refreshing milk to drink, but also fibrous pan-scouring pads from its husk, a biodegradable cobbled path renewed every year with the season's outer shells, and stripped leaves to weave into mats and baskets. Her calabash tree grew gourds which she dried and cleaned to fashion into bowls to contain fresh shrimps ready for cooking. Her nenwah, our English loofah, was cooked with the shrimps and never went near the bathroom!

When my grandmother visited us in the town, she would be laden with seasonal fruits and vegetables and lots of good things made from her garden, leaving me with a very desirable picture of plenty which inspired me to emulate the same abundance from whatever piece of land I had for my own garden.

When I came to England in 1959, I immediately realised that, at school, I had learned more about the Manchester Ship Canal than I had about British Guiana. The information on postage stamps on letters from my family was a revelation and made me long for space in which to create my own piece of home, just like any other exile from the ancient Romans up to today's asylum-seekers. After we were married, we rented a small terraced house with a back yard completely covered in concrete paving slabs - under a foot of snow when we moved in. As soon as it thawed, we lifted two slabs to expose half a square yard of soil which we improved to support a couple of outdoor tomato plants and companion marigolds. At that time it seemed to be more important for our hands to have direct contact with the earth than resort to the more obvious solution of container gardening. That would come later.

Whilst the stamps on letters from home made me dream of Victoria regia lilies, I was discovering unusual varieties of tomatoes like the Green Zebra.

When my husband completed his architectural studies at Liverpool University, we spent two years in a flat before buying our first house near Sefton Park. This had little more than a privet hedge in front from which my husband took an endless supply of twigs to make trees for his architectural models, having found that it would yield sizes to suit almost any scale. The back yard contained a small patch of bare earth which excited a Sudanese friend who could hardly wait to come back to plant coriander seeds without which life itself was just not possible. But this lack of space, together with a growing family, frustrated the deep-seated need to grow things myself. We befriended the custodian of the Sefton Park Palm House who presented to us a precious papaya he had nurtured because he had a daughter-in-law who was from tropical climes. Perhaps he gave her one, too?

We moved to Northampton to a terraced house having sufficient space which could be recognised as a potential garden. But with two small boys growing up fast, most of the space was a lawn immediately designated as a ball-field, leaving only a small area in which to plant a few vegetables. Our elder son became most excited when he found green caterpillars on the Brussels sprouts and demanded that we should get them some "caterpillow food"!? Children just love pets.

Corylus avellana
hazel nut tree

The arrival of their sister was an added deterrent to serious activity in the garden, so my husband often took the boys to Abington Park to let off steam. On one autumnal Sunday morning they were disappointed to find no conkers, but they quickly discovered that the park had so much more to offer. They studied every tree in the park in a search for different fruits and pods and came home with their bags full of walnuts, beech nuts, sweet chestnuts, planes, sycamores, catalpa beans and acorns from English and Turkey oaks. From this it was then a natural step to seek other treasures in local woods and hedgerows where we found blackberries, sloes, more sweet chestnuts and our first hazel nuts picked directly from the trees. These experiences introduced us to wild flowers and became a most formative influence on the future of our gardening as well as nurturing an embryo botanist who began to take a keen interest in everything he found growing anywhere.

At this time we began a lifelong love affair with Kew Gardens and made ritual visits two or three times every year. I would always make straight for the systematic beds, which attracted me like a magnet, as I always valued the lesson these taught the children about the incredible diversities which can exist within one family.

Before we could think of establishing a meaningful garden, my husband took a contract in Pakistan where we rented a bungalow in a very fashionable Housing Society in Karachi. The garden was blessed with a small collection of tropical plants which included two superb mango trees, bananas, a citrus lime, a tall spindle of a papaya, a bean tree, hibiscus bushes, roses and a fragrant "Queen of the Night" jasmine scrambling over the pergola outside the bedroom to give out its exotic perfume in the humid night air. Another indelible memory was the Callistemon holding, in her flamboyant red bottle brushes, the heat of lemon-scented days with a taste of foreign breezes which reminded me so much of my childhood in British Guiana.

The soil was almost pure desert sand and had to be treated regularly with "sweet earth", manure delivered by donkey cart to be distributed, dug in and watered by the "mali". Mali and our bearer, Mohammad Shafi, also built a lethal barrier of thorn branches as natural barbed wire to defend the crop from our two prize mango trees. This made up for Mali's picking of the bananas too early and nearly losing two whole stems laden with the spiralling hands of fruit. It was an absolute luxury for me to have a banana flower from another stem balanced in a vase in our dining room.

There were also potted plants which introduced us to the Asclepiadaceae family in the form of *Stapelia magna* which produced one ephemeral starfish flower with the most disgusting aroma, after which the plant died whether by neglect or from natural causes, I never knew.

The contract ended prematurely when war broke out with India at the end of 1971 and we returned to the depths of winter in England.

We settled in Barton Seagrave, a dormitory village of Kettering, and bought a post-war semi-detached house with lawns front and back, so our first purchase was a lawnmower to keep the grass under control while we came to terms with more land than we had ever owned before. The garden began by teaching us that our active children preferred to play ball on the other side of the fence with the children next door because their lawn was twice the size of ours. This left us free to think of "developing" a real garden for the first time. We took an approach which grew naturally rather than trying to design the whole layout in one go. The two-foot wide borders around the lawns were all enlarged to accommodate vegetables, flowers, an alpine rockery, a rose hedge, a cobbled patio, our own hazel trees, apples and pears. We also cut three small beds into the remains of the back lawn for the children to grow whatever interested them, so the lawn became little more than grassy paths between all these features and we had to buy shears to trim interminable edges.

In the front lawn we cut a crescent-shaped herb bed. For the first year the new plants looked beautiful, but gradually they all grew into each other, the more rampant varieties completely swamping those of a more delicate disposition. It soon looked a tangled mess and I learned that it is extremely difficult to manage a herb bed on a small scale if you wish to include a useful selection of plants - although a self-set corn poppy crowned this tangle with a display of 80 glorious red flowers. The front borders were remodelled to contain species roses and aromatic shrubs. I had no desire to plant anything which was already growing in neighbouring gardens, although it was necessary to observe what was there to determine what types of plants would be most likely to succeed. I always wanted to grow things that I couldn't see anywhere else, to grow a plant even to see it flower only once, just to say that I had seen it and knew its particular beauty. We put in annual spectaculars like sunflowers, artichokes, cardoons, painted lady runner beans, just to give the neighbours something to talk about. Wild strawberries crept in from next door and were made most welcome.

We made many expeditions to local woods, learned much about native plants and plant communities, and joined the Alpine Garden Society because alpine plants were habitually very small and a large number of different varieties could be accommodated in a small space. We found a mine of information in a garden centre half a mile down the road where a young Geoff Hamilton was busy writing about gardens but had not yet made his mark on television. I read gardening books by Joy Larkcom, H E Bates, Graham Stuart Thomas, Juliette de Bairacli Levy, Roy Genders. I studied all the garden catalogues from cover to cover, finding at the back of Thompson & Morgan's list the most exciting information but with no illustrations. So we acquired a large number of botanical books and field guides which increased my passion for studying plant families. I had struggled to grow plants of my tropical childhood because I could never give them the conditions they needed, so I sought other members of their families which I hoped might be easier to keep alive. Having killed so many Hoyas and Stephanotis, I learned that these were members of the Asclepiadaceae and it was a joy to discover that Chiltern Seeds offered seeds of a hardy *Asclepias syriaca* which I could grow outdoors. Our pool of knowledge was gradually building up as was our experimental garden. When we moved in 1984 we took over two hundred small pots of our treasures with us. We were now ready to do some serious gardening.

Pods of Asclepias syriaca *about to release their seeds.*

The Garden

sweet bay

We moved to Bedford when our children had all reached stages in their education which effectively enabled them to leave the nest and allow us to concentrate on other things. Our new home at "The Laurels" sounded grand but was an ordinary Victorian semi-detached town house about five minutes' walk from the market square and the medieval St Paul's church. At the west entrance to the church, are the Howard Memorial doors of engraved glass, depicting first woman Eve eternally tending her ripening grapes and wheat. These two plants were her first choice, though in reality all of earth was hers to choose from, so I believed they said much to us. Beautiful in their simplicity, they did not speak of awesome vistas with gazebos or other expensive garden artefacts on the horizon, nor of great Jekyllian swathes of coordinated colour. The grapes and wheat spoke to me of two people come upon hard times, needing to make wise decisions. Cast out from Paradise with no Angels to ease the task, their first priority was what to eat and drink. How clever, then, that they should have chosen such plants. Eve's hunger for the knowledge of the apple really would have enabled them to do some lateral thinking, finding many uses for only the two plants. The juice of grapes for wine, condiments, flavours; its leaves for the most gourmet of cooking; its tendrils and seeds for medicines; its vine strong enough for rope, for baskets. And what of wheat? Consider bread alone, in incredible variety throughout the world; straw for thatching, warm bedding and fodder for animals. All this and beauty too. Is there anything more beautiful than a grape vine in full fruit, or late sunshine on a field of ripening wheat? Their sin might have brought them down to earth, but I think it would also have led them to wonderful discoveries and magnificent harvests.

Grape vine decoration on a misericord seat in St Paul's Church, Bedford.

Whilst we were some way from creating our own Garden of Eden, or coming even close to my grandmother's Paradise, our new garden was more than the pocket-handkerchief of modern houses but smaller in terms of the manorial gardens which media-driven garden designers consider "small". But, having gardened with some interest and satisfaction on half a square yard of ground, I'd like to think that we were able to demonstrate, with all of its plants and their bonus activities, that size is not the most important thing. The act of gardening was what mattered, for to garden was to hold in our hands the substance of our own creation, the very stuff of stars. I believed it was an intimacy we involved in with our very being. To us, however, it provided a wonderful opportunity to create a garden to suit our needs in a space 50 feet long and 25 feet wide. It had a lawn and a vegetable border separated by a concrete path with a washing line tethered to a derelict shed, one ancient Worcester Pearmain apple tree and not a laurel in sight. Having acquired a house called "The Laurels", how could we not plant a bay tree, *Laurus nobilis*? The sheer romance of its leaves and berries, wreathed into crowns for poets, great orators and kings, made it irresistible. But this turned out to be one of those occasions when romance and practicality walked hand-in-hand. What flair it lent to my cooking: old leaves for winter stews, younger ones for meatballs, burgers, stir fries, sauces. Both of them ground as an essential ingredient for wet and dry pot-pourri. Deliciously medieval!

Ornamental Bay Laurel on Bedford Corn Exchange.

The back garden had the advantage of being enclosed and sheltered with a long south-facing brick wall to protect tender exotic plants which would struggle to survive elsewhere. The east end of the garden had another brick wall which was tucked beneath the canopy of next door's 70 feet high lime trees which stopped rain reaching the ground whilst their roots sucked out any remaining moisture. In these conditions we did manage to establish two marvellous hybrid musk roses and a white mulberry. The south border was in the shade of a concrete wall which absorbed the sun's warmth on its other side and radiated this into our garden to relieve the effects of dark winter shadows. The damper soil conditions gave scope for a different range of plants, including my new-found *Asclepias syriaca*, and ended in a very small kitchen garden outside the back door which gave shelter to many pots of herbs in its fallow periods.

The herbs were the lifeblood of the garden, my kitchen and my personal well-being. I learned that some herbs like coriander, thyme, garlic chives, balm of Gilead, came readily from seed, although basils needed a good healthy cursing to achieve any results. Others, like sage in all its varieties could be kept going from cuttings, as could the sweet bay and santolina. They could be picked and dried for winter storage at just the right time and could also be used as companion plants to protect more vulnerable species against pests and diseases. I depended on them for my immediate cosmetics and medicinal remedies. When the children were little, they believed that a herb tea or two really helped a cold or a temperature. And they would never be sad if I presented a salad decorated with the azure blue rockets of Borage.

The central area was planted with trees and evolved around a small woodland area of five hazels and ground cover of wild strawberries, pignuts and a selection of bulbs. On one side of this we planted a quince, *Cydonia oblonga*, like the four trees planted in the Tower of London in 1275, by which time the quince had already enjoyed a long history in England, thanks to the Roman occupation. For me, Edward Lear's owl and pussycat conjured up childhood images filled with a great curiosity and a desire to taste such delicacies for myself.

"...they dined on mince and slices of quince
which they ate with a runcible spoon..."

There is a Jewish tradition that the quince tree grew in the Garden of Eden and was the home of the serpent. In the ancient world of Greece and Rome, the quince was a symbol of happiness, love and fruitfulness and was dedicated to the goddess Venus. In 17th century Britain, the Tradescants introduced new varieties and "Portugal" is still available. Its profusion of dainty pink-flushed flowers in the spring is reminiscent of wild roses, and its large impressive pear-shaped fruits are the colour of new lemons. Its fragrance on ripening is the nearest thing, in an autumnal English garden, to the tropical scent of mangoes and, like mangoes, I prized it for cooking certain dishes, especially fish. This tree was a most rewarding link with our garden's Victorian past. I attempted to make quince jelly but this turned out to be "Carne de Membrillo" used by Spanish gypsies as a tonic, and it should have been spread to set in a shallow dish rather than allowed to solidify in a jar. I had more success with quince jam, using the whole pulp and the peel to produce a delicately aromatic preserve which came more readily out of the jar!

On the other side of our small copse we planted another fruit tree with historical connections, having been brought to England by King Richard the Lionheart. He had spent most of his ten year reign away at the Crusades which achieved, it is said, little more for England than the introduction of the apricot. This should not be underestimated as it was a tree used to enhance the cloister gardens of monasteries where the sequence of blossom, leafy shade and delicious fruits were valued attributes which satisfied all the medieval criteria of beauty, fragrance and usefulness, as indeed was our own tree which grew as a free-standing specimen rather than a cordon cossetted under protective screens against the wall. It relished its freedom by producing over two hundred large, juicy fruits in one season, and it grew at an alarming rate which kept us busy with a pruning saw.

We also tried to grow a medlar tree in a large pot which we kept at the front of the house. One night, this disappeared along with all the hanging baskets in the road! But we did enjoy the fruits of a large Russian variety begged from an exhibitor at an RHS show in Westminster.

There were still small spaces in the garden for more roses. My father had told me that they gathered roses in India to make Attar and his words created within me entrancing and enduring images, and if I could, I would gather all the roses of the world and live my entire life amongst them. So all of my roses, about thirty in all, were chosen for their perfume. We also made a scree bed for bulbs and grasses with a main feature of a spectacular Bromiliad, *Fascicularia bicolor* with its technicolour flowers and spiny-toothed foliage. But, having filled all available space, our need for annual vegetables presented a problem after our initial allotment bed had become a small lawn for occasional relaxation. After a pilgrimage to Potato Day at the Henry Doubleday Research Association, Ryton, most of our paving was covered with 30 assorted tubs and buckets awaiting the harvesting of so many different varieties to the amazement of our grandchildren to whom the search for potatoes in the compost was like hunting buried treasure. Peas, beans, tomatoes, courgettes, wonderful American squashes and lots of other desirable things to eat were planted in a grand assortment of containers. And as more plants moved into pots, I gained yet another activity in training them, as naturally as possible, to live within their allotted space, becoming akin to little pets. Like everything else connected with the garden, this was a most peaceful and rewarding pastime.

All the diverse conditions within a relatively small space enabled us to experiment with a wide variety of plants. Any which could not be accommodated in the ground or needed to be moved around according to the seasons were planted in pots. Many began life in our distinctive cold frame, a "Growmate" rotating pyramid, which our grandchildren affectionately called "the rocket" - an ideal vehicle for a Time Lord to give our unusual plants a headstart in life.

The narrow spaces between the houses presented a different challenge and became our secret garden where some exotics, including a Camellia, were persuaded to thrive in the shelter but with limited direct sunlight. This linked to the front garden, a small oasis of surprises, bounded by a low hedge made from cuttings of Buxus from my collection of little pets. Within this enclosure, various specimen plants could be relied upon to turn heads and become conversation pieces with enthusiastic passers-by who were always ready to stop and exchange information on plants. The bay window overlooking the front garden served as a greenhouse in which we created a small piece of Guyana with plants such as Bougainvillea, Stephanotis, sambac jasmine, cotton, a few lesser-known passion flowers and a Gloriosa Lily given to me by our son's Professor of Botany at Bangor University.

Shetland Black Potatoes

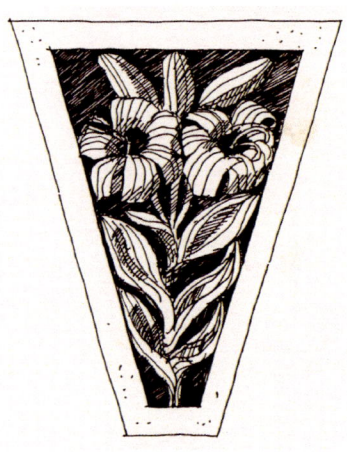

And so, with an understanding of our new garden, and with many other thoughts in mind, I chose my plants, each one for its many virtues. And further, not just for the garden as an entity in itself, but for the home and the family which I believed to be integral parts of a greater whole. I did this not only as Eve might have done, but also in the spirit of medieval gardeners, though unlike me they organised their beds with practicality and strict discipline. What we have in common is the criterion of plant use in daily life, and it is interesting just how much evidence of this exists all around us, especially in the botanical ornamentation of buildings from the grapes on the medieval misericords in St Paul's church to the Madonna lilies on doorways on Victorian houses.

Our botanical library was expanding and Abbie Zabar's "The Potted Herb" was an inspiration, dedicated to "all those who want a little garden in their lives". My interest broadened to potted herbs which are indeed microcosms of gardens in containers and, like any "real" garden, this was no instant activity. The rewards came from long periods of nurturing, coaxing, loving, being given absolute personal attention, to be individually groomed like the cat, being transformed by a "makeover" into a distinct personality.

After attending a lecture on the Cloisters Museum by Bonnie Young at the RHS in London, we visited New York and headed straight for the northern tip of Manhattan where it is located. Medieval architectural details have been incorporated in modern buildings around a series of four courtyard gardens with a truly medieval feel. Bonnie Young's book "A walk through the Cloisters" became yet another inspiration for my evolving approach to gardening.

Plants were an essential part of our response to the seasons, and the winter was a time of anticipation as we waited for the winter aconites, nodding snowdrops, hellebores, early irises, *Clematis balearica*, *Lonicera fragrantissimma*, to receive our emotional exclamations when they faithfully appeared, each in its turn dispensing beauty as though it were limitless. Their magnanimity and fortitude was always a lesson to me because they gave so much in hard times.

On a philosophical level we tried to adopt the medieval principles of growing plants which are useful, fragrant or beautiful, preferably all three at the same time. Many fruits and vegetables could certainly be beautiful, but their uses were not always restricted to the obvious culinary applications. Herbs could also be cosmetic or medicinal. Fragrant plants used in perfumery could also be applied to incense, beads, decorative arrangements, wreaths and swags, as well as in traditional pot-pourri. Many of our plants yielded fibres or other materials for making paper, fabrics, baskets. Beauty could also mean interesting and we learned that there were many ways to please the senses - especially the sense of wonder and, occasionally, even the sense of humour.

With our collection of plants expanding and our knowledge of their uses increasing, we began to explore the traditional uses of various plants beyond the more obvious utilitarian, culinary, cosmetic and medicinal. We dried leaves, collected pods and seeds, soaked stems to remove fibres, left them over winter for the frosts to help in the process, employed kitchen gadgets for purposes not entirely connected with cooking to complete the work. When we processed plant materials for one purpose, we found that the residue could often be used for another. Having experimented with stems and leaves of *Hibiscus cannabina, Cedronella triphylla, Asclepias syriaca, Medicago arborea* in making different recipes for paper, we were intrigued by the various colours in the liquid left over. This was the beginning of further experiments with natural dyes. But dyes need fabrics and we could have waited forever to grow enough cotton to spin on our 'charka', attempting to rise to Gandhi's exhortation to the Indian people in his campaign for Independence that they should spend some time each day spinning cotton. The 'charka' was invented to make this a feasible proposition and is a portable spinning wheel which folds into a box no larger than a book.

Instead, we took a short step to discover the art of making watercolours from the dyes, although the science of this was more akin to alchemy. These experiences added another dimension to the choice of new plants for the garden. We grew *Rubia tinctoria* for three years before harvesting the madder roots in the hope that we might learn the secrets of Turner and Constable who would mix their own colours from natural pigments.

None of these activities was ever intended to be developed as a consuming passion because we never considered ourselves to be "experts" as experts tend to take themselves too seriously. I did not want to do that because I believed too much in the joy of plants, in the spirit of plants and in the idea of green and growing things. It was the seemingly endless variety of the experiences which inspired us. By learning about the plants and what it was possible to make from them, we hoped that we could demonstrate that a garden was not just a place in which to mow lawns and weed flower beds. A garden is always a living thing, even with a garden full of plants, and change was often necessary when circumstances took it in unexpected directions. It had to respond to the demands of grandchildren whose only desire was to dig holes. Plants died - not because of the holes - and needed to be replaced with something more robust. We were getting older and began to suffer more than the plants, so we began to think of down-sizing to a "no-maintenance" garden rather than just "low-maintenance". It was the gardeners who were becoming static, not the garden.

We still have wonderful memories of our investment of so much of our lives in the garden and its plants, and the proof of this rests in our children. Our first son, a reluctant botanist more interested in his "real" art to the extent that it was left to his father to record the plants, still brings back seeds and pods from holidays all over the world to produce yet more plants. Our second son can abandon the observation of his meteorological data in the far reaches of northern Scotland to bring me back, in his sandwich box, cotton grass the colour of old Victorian wedding dresses. Our daughter walks around with her head full of every rose I've ever grown and gives them to her son.

The Drawings

santolina

Our collection of plants was a product of our growing library of books about plants. The seed catalogues without pictures and with hardly any background information fired a quest for knowledge which could only be answered by more and more books. Botanical tomes helped to relate plants within their families and, before long, this knowledge generated a need to find more sources for the cousins, the uncles, the aunts and more distant relatives, so plantsmen's lists were added to the seed catalogues. The geographical distribution needed to be understood if successful germination or propagation was going to be achieved and the precious seedling might have a chance of surviving. Then the social and cultural history of the plants was discovered in ancient herbals, missals, books of hours, diaries of intrepid plant hunters; florilegia of royal gardens, bishops' gardens, aristocratic gardens; garden magazines based on the work of select bands of illustrators; field guides with careful sketches and photographs. We learned that the Renaissance provoked a considerable scientific curiosity in plants, especially new discoveries from the expanding world with its various new empires. We visited Leiden and its historic botanical garden where the botanist Clusius became Professor of Natural Sciences in 1593. He experimented with many of these plants and set out his garden with systematic beds, but in order to be able to instruct his students throughout the year, he also gathered contemporary illustrations for publication by the Plantin Press of Antwerp to provide him with a florilegium which became his "winter garden" for this purpose.

The 17th century Dutch "flower piece" took a more artistic view, ignoring the science, and gathered together plants which were in flower at different times and so expressed the love which collectors had to preserve a collection by recording them at their best. The paintings would outlive the original specimens - and, in the end, would cost much less.

As we gathered all this material which divulged intimate details about our plants, it gradually germinated into a passion to produce our own florilegium.

We had our favourites and some of these were studied in some detail, especially if the plants showed potential for being beautiful, useful and fragrant. Prime amongst these were the Asclepiadaceae of my childhood. *Stephanotis floribunda* was perhaps the most nostalgic as its scent took me right back to being a small child wandering under an arbour, loving the secrecy, and it was my size because I could reach my hands up and touch the luscious seed pods hanging there, waiting to burst and release parachutes of fine silk threads. That was sheer magic. But it was *Asclepias syriaca* which became a real treasure because its scent was so much like the Stephanotis. We learned that this plant and its cousins provided the defensive milky sap to protect the Monarch butterflies in their seasonal progress across North America from Mexico to Canada. In our garden it was small blue fritillary butterflies which found the flowers irresistible. It grew and spread with abandon on its subterranean runners but we didn't mind. Who could object to walking between hedges of dusky pink flowers, buzzing with bees and filling the air with the most exotic perfume in the twilight of a hot summer evening? In good years, I loved to watch the swelling of up to eight or ten pods on each stem until they finally burst to release a generosity of seeds on the flimsiest of gossamer silk parachutes which I gathered to make experimental felt. But there was more to be done with the spent plants: the thin bark was carefully stripped to make coils for constructing baskets and, when the milky sap had dried enough, the stems were shredded to make pulp for paper. Then we found ways to use the residual liquid for dyes and paints. The dried seed pods were fixed into swags and wreaths to remind us of the glory of the plant until next year's crop.

This, all-in-all, was a very satisfying plant and its close cousins *A.purpurascens* and *A.curassavica*, although less dynamic, were equally loved, as were more distant relatives *Oxypetalum caeruleum* and *Vincetoxicum nigrum* which also made silk in its pods, quite like little canoes when they opened. *Hoya bella* and *Hoya carnosa* were available in local garden centres, but occasionally we found more unusual varieties like *Hoya lacurosa* and *Hoya multiflora*. We continued to add specimens to this family and our last acquisition was a *Ceropegia sandersonii* from a visit to the Copenhagen Botanic garden in 2002.

It is perhaps surprising that this family is not represented in the selection of drawings which follows, but it is inevitable that there will always be some plants which do not fit comfortably into convenient pigeon-holes. How, after all, do you choose a theme when the number of illustrations needs to be limited to only a small proportion of the whole collection? The annual emergence of winter aconites suggested a seasonal theme to demonstrate the time-shifting nature of the garden, but this did not provide sufficient opportunity to capture all the magic of plants that, say, a selection of 80 drawings, emulating Philleas Fogg's journey around the world, seemed to offer. However, this was more than would be feasible to mount as an exhibition at the Royal Horticultural Society's winter shows. Even 26 drawings of a garden alphabet seemed to be pushing the limits if these were to be drawn in the natural size of the plants to comply with the Society's requirements. By making the drawings small, it was still possible to draw the details of the specimens in their natural size although the overall character of the plants was, to some extent, sacrificed to achieve this. But then, gardening itself cannot always be practised without some degree of compromise? So an alphabetical list of plants was drawn up with criteria which embraced medieval beauty, fragrance and usefulness, added to the desire to represent every corner of the world and all of them to be selected from plants which had travelled through space and time to bring their magic to a small town garden in Bedford.

Between 1990 and 2001 the collection of drawings in our florilegium expanded to nearly 400 specimens. Around 170 of these were exhibited at Royal Horticultural Society flower shows in Westminster, gaining awards of twelve medals, five of these being silver-gilt. The early exhibitions were on general themes of climbers and flowering shrubs, then as our collections of plant families grew to significant numbers, they concentrated on the specific families of Irises, Roses, Asclepiadaceae, Solanaceae, Malvaceae, Papaveraceae and Salvias, returning later to collections of fruit and vegetables and culminating in a study of plants whose roots were used for a variety of purposes. Over 800 different specimens of our plants were captured on photographic slides, indicating that the potential to develop more themes, or to extend those already started, was increasing faster than they could be drawn. Seeds of cyclamen were drawn, waiting for next year's flowers.

The modest research it took to investigate our selection of plants revealed all sorts of other interesting information apart from the geography of their distribution. So many of them had historical and cultural associations as well as their more obvious culinary, medicinal and economic uses. The outcome was a list of plants which turned our small garden into a virtual time machine! From the history of the Bible, ancient Egyptians, Greeks and Romans, we moved through the mysteries of medieval apothecaries' workshops of medicine, alchemy and perfumery, reflected on the colonisation of the New World and the economics of the slave trade, indulged in the romance of Victorian plant hunters and even learned of the poisons employed by a 20th century murderer. The drawings give only a brief glimpse of the garden but hopefully express more than a suggestion of the philosophy which generated it, illustrating a collection of plants, along with their histories, their uses and their beauties, brought together to enrich the lives of a couple of ageing gardeners and their family. An Earthstar, *Geastrum triplex,* appeared miraculously in the bark mulch beneath the apricot tree and demonstrated that magic can occur in the most unexpected places at any time.

Arisarum

Arisarum proboscidium is a diminutive member of the Aroid family. It's so cute that I'm always inspired to pick up a tail and surprise a little mouse. Hence its common name of Mousetail plant. It is a plant with a definite sense of humour.

The first hint that it may be in flower is the sight of a mass of long purple tails peeping out from beneath a low umbrella of glossy, green, hastate leaves, suggesting that indeed there might be a colony of small mice inside, plotting mischief. There is an irresistible urge to eavesdrop, and what you find, when you stoop down to part the leaves, is a covern of purplish brown, white-throated flowers for all the world like hooded witches gathered together for something far more sinister. At this point, just try and see if you can stop smiling?

The plant's natural habitat is the wild woods of Italy and Spain. In our garden it prospered in the shade of the north-facing wall, beneath the canopy of the hazel tree copse. It flowers in early spring and by midsummer it has totally disappeared until the next year.

Billardiera

The stories of plants are often closely linked to the stories of the plant hunters who discovered them. A A Anderson's tale of Citizen Labillardiere in his little book, "The Coming of the Flowers", tells of a botanical expedition to the South Pacific and Australia at the end of the 18th century. As a consequence of the French Revolution, he became separated from his specimens and, by the time he made his way back to France, those specimens were being held as prizes of war in Britain. Sir Joseph Banks, who had been on similar expeditions with Captain Cook, appreciated the rigours of plant collecting, so he arranged for the specimens to be returned to the man who had so risked his life gathering them, insisting that he should receive the glory for their discovery.

Amongst the plants was *Billardiera longiflora*, named in his honour. This delightful small evergreen climber was introduced to Britain in 1810 from Tasmania and New South Wales. We grew it in a pot which stood outside our back door, facing south, where it survived very decoratively for three years. Its stems, which seem so fragile, are in fact very wiry and the wonderful metallic indigo berries give it its common name of Purple Apple Berry. I had so looked forward to tasting these tempting "edible" fruits but was totally disappointed. It was a lesson in how to interpret plant descriptions: edible does not mean tasty, rather it indicates that death does not follow from eating it! The berries were bland to the degree of being tasteless and are not worth eating - unless you are stranded on a desert island with no other option. But their colour is out of this world, so I had no regrets for growing this quietly delightful plant.

Corylus

Corylus avellana and *C.maxima* are the hazels, cobs and filberts which formed the structure of the small woodland area in the centre of our garden. These reminded us of days when we took our young children to the woods to collect fallen nuts and they determined to have their own hazel copse. It was a great leap to look forward to gathering the harvest with our grandchildren in our own garden - and share the nuts with the neighbourhood squirrel. The nodding yellow catkins brightened the bare garden throughout the winter until we saw the first, insignificant, red flowers open on the branches waiting for the wind to deliver the pollen. The effect of coppicing kept the stools small enough for our limited space whilst still creating the impression of a small wood from only five multi-stemmed trees. Grown commercially in France, Spain, Italy, Turkey and Oregon in USA ,the trees can yield up to half a ton of nuts per acre. The nuts are crushed to produce an oil used in foods, perfumery, soaps and paints. Leaves are occasionally used as tobacco substitutes. We used the stems to provide good straight sticks for making pyramids to support peas and beans, but we did not venture into charcoal-making as a step towards homemade gunpowder!

We have picked hazel nuts from the woods in Bedfordshire and Northamptonshire, from the Burren in Ireland and even from the trees outside Marple swimming pool. At the right time, the nuts are sweet and succulent, and a marvellous addition to our diet. But the nicest thing about our own hazels was what we grew beneath them in their dappled shade. Remembering the pleasures of gathering wild strawberries in a Lake District wood, we could enjoy our own wild and alpine varieties until the frosts ended the season. We also colonised lesser and greater pignuts in the hope that they might one day yield a worthwhile crop. Amongst these we also planted fritillaries and even a common spotted orchid, rescued long ago, with permission from British Rail, from an abandoned railway line before it became a bypass.

The true hazel is a British native plant, the filbert with its longer nuts was an introduction from the Balkans in 1759. Archeological studies have established that hazel nuts had their origins as a source of food in the Mesolithic period of the Stone Age around nine thousand years ago.

Datura

We grew many plants from the Solanaceae family and we were constantly inspired by the family's diversity, ranging as it does from the very poisonous to the supremely edible - and tasty - and just about everything in between. Some of them are highly decorative whilst others are indispensible to us in our daily lives.

Datura stramonium is commonly called the Thorn Apple because of its spiny seed capsule. It is mainly cultivated for the several alkaloids, including scopolamine, atropine and daturine, which it yields from its seeds, flowers and foliage. The "knockout drops" made from this have been used by thieves and assassins in India to stupify or kill their victims. It has been used by Indian tribes as a narcotic in their initiation ceremonies for boys entering manhood, and it is believed to have been used by the ancient Greek priests of Delphos to produce the paroxysms they attributed to Divine power, as did the ancient Peruvians on the other side of the globe. On the positive side, it can be used medicinally to treat asthma and bronchial complaints.

In the Old World its distribution includes North Africa and Southern Europe. After its introduction into North America it became known as Jimson Weed, a corruption of Jamestown, the first English settlement in Virginia in 1603, where it grew prolifically. It is an annual and, in those years when we grew it, it intrigued all who saw it. The repetitive geometry of the plant is fascinating, and the development of the branches could well have been the inspiration for the study of modern fractal patterns.

Eschscholzia

There was hardly a member of the Papaveraceae family that did not immediately fill me with inexpressible admiration on sight. They are, one and all, so stunning in the simplicity of their structure and so innocent, yet so resplendent in their display, that no gardener could desire more of them than that they exist.

Eschscholzia californica is no exception to this, being a delightfully elegant plant to grace any garden. Our exotic hybrids, bought at great expense from commercial seedsmen, were no more beautiful than those with startlingly silken orange petals which seeded themselves in the joints of the brick paving in our front drive. In the face of such generosity, I was tempted to hope that they might have multiplied enough to enable me to try them, in the manner of the Indian tribes of south-west USA, as a vegetable. Or, as the Spanish Californians do, to fry the whole plant in olive oil, not to eat, but by adding perfume to create a highly-prized hair oil which is said to promote hair growth. Perhaps this would have made a useful supplement to a gel I made from simmering 30 seeds from quince fruit for 15 minutes in a quarter of a pint of water to make a wonderful setting lotion or gel from the mucilage which is released. The Arabs used brewed peel from the quince to improve the manes and tails of their magnificent Arabian thoroughbred horses. Mere mortals could also try scraping the thick down from young leaves and fruits to mix with honey to apply to the scalp as a hair restorer?

Feijoa

Feijoa sellowiana is a monotypic summer-flowering genus of a small evergreen tree belonging to the Myrtaceae family. It grew well against our south-facing wall, and in good seasons it produced amongst its grey-green leaves with their white-felted undersides, many of its spectacular, exotic flowers with their multitude of showy stamens so typical of this family. Sadly, without a suitable pollinator, it never produced an egg-shaped fruit, although we did buy one in a local supermarket and discovered how the plant got its common name of Fruit Salad Bush. On this I hung impossible dreams of ripe guavas from the "Land of Many Waters" - Guyana - of which this plant, beautiful in its own right, reminded me. I would have given it twice the space just for that memory. However, we were amply compensated because the crimson and white waxy petals were good to eat, having a rich aromatic flavour which, in our opinion, transformed a very ordinary green salad into something very gourmet - when we found the will to actually pick them!

The plant was discovered by Friedrich Sellow while he was plant-hunting in Brazil and Uruguay from 1821 to 1829. However, its generic name commemorates a minor Portugese botanist, Joas da Silva Feijo. It was introduced to Britain in 1898 but in its native habitat it is grown for its fruits which are eaten raw or made into preserves, which for us remained a dream.

Gossypium

Gossypium hirsutum of the Malvaceae family, is the American Upland cotton which produces both long and short staple fibres in USA. Because of its high cellulose content it can also be used to make paper and artificial silk, oil from its seeds for making margarine, soap, cosmetics, candles and lubricating oil and cellulose for industrial production, with residual seedcake being fed to cattle. The fact that we were able to grow a specimen for the drawing is proof of the saying "nothing ventured, nothing gained". Having no greenhouse facilities, it was always asking the impossible to grow tropical and sub-tropical plants from seed. It took five years to produce one plant, trying seed from various sources. Though our plant made many wonderful flowers and promising pods, only one expanded and burst to reveal a proper boll. In spite of this, we kept trying hoping that we might eventually be rewarded by a wealth of wonderful bolls of our own cotton to spin on our Gandhian 'charka'. But this was not to be.

The history of cotton is inspiring and intriguing, having been grown in the Indus Valley before 3000BC and in Peru before 2500BC. The word cotton is derived from the Arabic 'kutun' and the term muslin comes from the town of Mosul in Iraq where the cloth was first made. In the 16th century, many Europeans believed that cotton came from a tiny 'vegetable lamb' that grew on trees. Indian cotton was introduced to Europe by the Venetians who set up a monopoly and organised camel trains to Italy. To avoid importing cotton from India, the British set up cotton plantations in the Caribbean and North America with seeds from Indian plants. In 1732 they also introduced upland cotton from seeds produced in the Chelsea Physic Garden. In America, cotton began as the crop of the poor white settlers, but an increased demand created a need for more intensive picking and ginning of the cotton to remove the seeds. Machine harvesting reduced the quality as the pods do not all ripen at the same time and leaves were also gathered, so the solution to this problem was to import slaves to carry out the work, initiating a barbarous trade in human beings. While the American South became dependent upon slaves, the textile trade in Britain produced mill towns which were wholly populated by wage slaves, mainly women and children because mill owners could pay them lower wages. Their lot did not improve even after the American Civil War effectively ended slavery in the cotton fields.

Hyoscyamus

Hyoscyamus niger, commonly known as the Black Henbane, is another member of the Solanaceae family. It is cultivated mainly in Russia, Germany and the United Kingdom for the alkaloids hyoscyamine and hyoscine which are contained in its leaves and flowering tops. These are much valued drugs in the treatment of various diseases of the bladder, asthma and severe pain. They are also sufficiently narcotic and hypnotic to have made the growing of the plant a minor industry in the Mitcham market gardens of south London where peppermint and lavender were also grown from 1750 to 1880, and watercress beds survived until after the Second World War. So impressive is its history that Mrs Grieve devotes some five pages of her "Modern Herbal" to its intricate description.

There is an amusing story in Brian Morley's "Wild Flowers of the World" which tells of the 19th century Scottish botanist, Boswell Syme's account of some monks who had mistakenly eaten roots of henbane and had become very confused and disorientated: one rang the bell for matins at midnight and of those who responded, some could read, others fancied the letters on the page were running about like ants, and some read what they did not find in their books. But it was perhaps more famously - or infamously - used by Dr Crippen to murder his wife in 1910, giving him the distinction of becoming the first murderer to be apprehended by the use of wireless telegraphy as he was making his escape on board a transatlantic liner.

Although it is a dangerously poisonous plant, we liked to grow it for its strange, almost sinister beauty, and our son having brought us seed from Padua, we also took great pleasure in growing the white variety whose flowers are smaller and more delicate, but quite as interesting.

Iris

In Greek mythology, the goddess Iris was a messenger of the Gods and displayed a rainbow as her sign. On a Crusade in the 12th century, King Louis VII chose the iris as his emblem and called it "Fleur de Louis". This became the symbol of France as "Fleur de Lys" and from 1339 to 1800 it appeared in the English Royal Arms. *Iris sibirica* has many cultivars ranging in colour from white to all shades of blue and deep indigo. In the wild, it spreads from eastern Europe, across Russia to the west of Lake Baikal and grows in wet meadows, damp forest margins and light deciduous woodland. Our cultivar was "Dragonfly", a stately slender plant in all its features, with fine narrow leaves which remained upright in all weathers. It was so impressive in our garden that, when its stand became exhausted, we were inspired to commemorate its elegance in some way. We harvested its leaves to make a small basket woven onto a base of wood from our acacia tree which had perished in a hard frost after only four years. This was a success and led us to experiment with the broader leaves of *Iris foetidissima*, the British native gladwin which I thought of as a most uninhibited plant, not at all shy to display its red seeds bursting out of dried pods. Using traditional rushwork technology, we made more baskets and a splendid garden hat, now in the Hatworks Museum in Stockport.

I had a great curiosity in plants connected with perfumery. It was an ambition fulfilled to have found and grown the orris root of *Iris florentina*, an important plant with a long commercial history of use in toilet powders, toothpaste and perfumes, especially those with a violet base. We grew it for two years then dried the roots for two years before it was ready to be carved into aromatic beads, with the shavings to be ground into a powder for a fixative in perfumery.

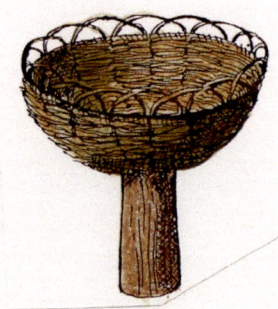

Job's Tears

Job's Tears, *Coix lacryma-jobi*, is a grass of the millet type cultivated throughout the tropics. It is a plant which enticed me not only for its usefulness but also for its decorative qualities. But, most of all, it was a plant of my Guyanese childhood. I remember it growing by the side of streams, tempting children to reach out for its alluring beads which appear in a variety of colours growing in the same inflorescence. Our seeds came from a rattle made from a dried gourd brought from Guyana as an Amerindian souvenir. We were delighted that they grew in our garden to make enough beads to be threaded into necklaces with fragrant beads of ground rose petals, blue glass beads and red ceramic discs. We also used the leaves, together with other plant material, to make paper.

In Papua New Guinea, tribal men wear the stems through their noses, and widows cover themselves in heavy necklaces made of the seeds, stripping the strands one at a time over many months until the end of their mourning period.

In east Asia the parched seeds are ground into flour. In China the seeds are used as a diuretic and the Japanese make a tea from the parched seeds.

Kalmia

Kalmia angustifolia is a low, thicket-forming shrub from eastern North America. It is a member of the Ericaceae family and its common name of Sheep Laurel was one of the reasons which attracted us to it, because our home being called "The Laurels" inspired us to grow any plant which carried that name - even with the limitations of space in our small garden. In the event, the plant did not prosper, even in a pot of ericaceous compost, although it survived for a few years until it was broken by the weight of heavy snow, leaving only the topiary bay laurel to uphold the name of the house. But it did survive long enough to produce its flowers with their fascinating construction of ten stamens emerging from the centre of the flower, sprung like ribs of an umbrella into sockets in the middle of the petals from where they are released to scatter pollen over visiting insects. It has a most dainty appearance, being smaller in all aspects than the more flamboyant Calico Bush, *K.latifolia*.

The plant was introduced to Britain in 1736 by John Bartram, the first American-born plant hunter who explored Indian territory from Florida to Canada. Its roots were used to make tobacco pipes, and its wood sometimes carved into household articles such as spoons, which earned it the Indian name of Spoonwood.

Loasa

Every year we had a great deal of fun seeking out any unusual annuals in the new seed catalogues. They provided an added excitement to the gardening year while we waited and wondered if we would succeed in discovering what these unusual plants would look like. We originally grew *Loasa vulcanica* under its synonym *Blumenbachia rosenbachianum* and it is one of the most intriguing plants we ever experienced. It is a tangled, twining plant, with hairy leaves, hairy stems, hairy seed pods and even hairy flowers. But beware of it! Every one of these hairs can sting without hesitation if you so much as touch it, even when the plant has been uprooted and hung up to dry, when it still continues to flower. The pods can still sting after years of storage. It is these pods which have given the plant its common name of "Mosque Plant" from their spiralling spheres reminiscent of the Islamic domes of Samarkand. They unwind very sensuously to release their seeds, given the right conditions.

It was first discovered by Berthold Carl Seeman in Ecuador, but was not introduced to Britain until 1876 when it was rediscovered by Edouard Francois Andre who bitterly recorded being stung fiercely by the plant while collecting it. Perhaps, if he had taken the time to look around, he might have found an antidote plant, much as our native dock always seems to grow near to stinging nettles?

This was our introduction to the family Loasaceae , and over the years we managed to grow more members of the family. *Loasa triphylla* has similar flowers but is an upright plant with larger leaves. *Eucnide sp.* has yellow flowers, as does *Bartonia aurea*. The closest in character to the Mosque Plant is the *Cajophora sp.* with larger salmon-coloured flowers on a twining vine and seed pods with spiralling grooves on a long conical capsule. These all entertained us from year to year, just to see which varieties displayed the same hostile tendencies to sting the unwary.

Myrtus

Myrtus communis is the common myrtle, but what a travesty to call it so! Its flowers, though small, have an open, unpretentious beauty which leaves you deeply aware of honesty and innocence. I fell in love with it in the herb garden laid out in the Benedictine cloister of Peterborough Cathedral. The exquisite, sweet scent of the myrtle made it a natural companion to my quaint Rosemary Rose, the gorgeous Felicia Rose and the most dainty and unusual *Lavendula dentata* to make a pot-pourri, so on the dreariest of winter days I could open my pot and set free the scents of high summer.

It is a small tree with dense foliage, of Biblical origins, growing in damp plains of the River Jordan. Its leaves are used in Jewish betrothal rites and festivals, and it was also used by the ancient Egyptians and Romans. The Greeks celebrated it in their rituals, art and poetry, dedicating it to Aphrodite, the Goddess of love, beauty and fertility. The generic name may be derived from the Greek 'myron', meaning myrrh because of its fragrance and high, sweet-scented oil content. It was cultivated in England in the 16th century, and Queen Victoria popularised it by planting a sprig from her wedding bouquet in the grounds of Osborne House. She must have been a devoted gardener to allow herself to be distracted from the novelty of being a new bride to think about striking cuttings, even from a plant as beautiful as the myrtle?

But the legend which inspired me the most was that of Adam and Eve who, on leaving Eden, were allowed to take three things from the garden. They chose the date as the best of all fruits, a grain of wheat as the best of all foods, and a sprig of myrtle as the best of all fragrances. This is echoed in the medieval criteria of beauty, fragrance and usefulness by which I selected the plants for my garden. According to Islamic tradition, Adam took only the myrtle, and the great esteem in which Muslims held it is evidenced by the myrtle hedges in the courtyards of the Alhambra Palace in Granada.

The purple-black berries can be used as a condiment and we have used them to give a subtle flavour to roast lamb. They are also used medicinally to relieve stomach upsets, and an oil distilled from them makes a tonic. The hard wood is used for furniture, tool handles and walking sticks.

Nandina

Nandina domestica is all romance. It is a curious monotypic genus which could easily fool anyone into thinking that it is a bamboo. It is, in fact, a relative of the familiar garden plant, the Berberis, both being members of the Berberidaceae family. But because of its appearance it is known as the "Sacred Bamboo", and folklore has it that it is a great listener. If you tell the plant of your nightmares, it will despatch them in such a way that they will never return. I was asked if I did this, but had to admit that I had not so far done so, but I could foresee a day when I might be tempted to go out in the dead of night to talk to the plant and the neighbours would probably think I had gone completely mad. But why not try it? After all, just tell the plant your problem with no need for nasty medicines and no unpleasant side-effects!

It is an extremely decorative, medium height shrub, with bronze young leaves and slender, erect unbranched stems. The flowers are very small and numerous arranged in large terminal panicles, the individual petals having the strange texture of hard scales. They are a delicate mixture of pale yellow and white, a distinct treat for close-up examination. Our plant, having flowered for many months, still had three new panicles ready to open in November.

It was introduced to Britain in 1804 from central China and Japan where the wood is sometimes used to make chopsticks - which we never tried, not wishing to remove valuable stems from our plant.

Okra

The okra, *Hibiscus esculentus*, is a member of the Malvaceae family and a native of central Africa. It owes much of its distribution into the New World to its association with the slave trade. Sugar cane, taken to the West Indies during the Renaissance, was cultivated on plantations by black African slaves, as was cotton in north America. With the slaves came the okra, gumbo, lady's fingers, bindi, as it is variously called by the different ethnic groups who value it as a vegetable. The wide range of recipes exploits the essential characteristics of the pods in that slow cooking in stews releases the mucilaginous juices but quick stir-frying subdues this in favour of a delicious crunchy texture, thus appealing to all tastes. In my country of Guyana, it is a common plant in gardens, being very easy to grow and providing copious pods for the kitchen, though my mother could hardly have found many since my little brother and I were very fond of eating the raw fruit in its younger stage. It also made very attractive produce with which to stock our childhood shop to sell to neighbourhood children.

I remember also that if anyone had a scalp problem of any sort, such as dandruff, the fresh leaves would be macerated and made into a cold tea for washing the head. The mucilaginous pods are said to be good for upset stomachs and, when immature, can be made into a decoction for treating eye complaints, catarrh and inflamation of the reproductive system. The seeds can be used as a substitute for coffee and, considering all the delicious ways in which the pods can be used in cooking meats, curries and stews, it is no wonder it is so popular. The whole plant, including pods and roots are very fibrous and can be used for making paper. In Bedford, without a greenhouse, I always found it difficult to grow more than a few plants in pots, but I was happy if one actually flowered and ecstatic if it made even a single pod.

Papaver

Papaver somniferum is the Opium Poppy which has a long history as a medicinal and narcotic plant from the time of the ancient Egyptians up to the present day when the destruction of fields of poppies in Afghanistan has become a controversial political issue. It is a real pity that such a beautiful, ephemeral flower which unfolds so magically from its drooping bud capsule, like a conjuror's silk handkerchief, should be primarily associated in our minds with addiction to opium and heroin connected with organised crime on a grand scale. It is easy to lose sight of the fact that the crude opium obtained from the latex extracted from unripe seed capsules yields some 25 different alkaloids, some of which are indispensable to medicine. Morphine cannot be synthesised chemically so opium poppies are its only source, and where would we be without morphine and codeine for pain relief and sedation? Morpheus was the Greek god of dreams, and sleep was regarded as the greatest healer so the poppy was used to celebrate him in art, literature and religion.

In the 19th century, laudanum, a solution of opium in spirits of wine, was much used instead of tea by the much distressed urban poor in Britain, whilst the East India Company was trading opium with the Chinese for silver bullion, silk and real tea. The Company's manipulative activities eventually led to the Opium Wars of 1839-42.

Heroin, developed chemically from morphine, was found to be more effective and was sold commercially in the United States until 1917. By then, however, the social problems created by its abuse were deeply established. Today's illegal market is supplied from the Golden Crescent of Iran, Afghanistan and Pakistan.

More positively, the seeds, which contain no opium, are used to produce poppy seed oil used in curries and sweetmeats, paints, varnishes and soaps. The oil is also used in salad dressings in France and Germany and for lighting in India. The seedcake is valuable as cattle fodder. When a Pakistani friend had a headache, she ate all the seeds from one of my decorative home-grown pods and promptly recovered. Surely this is a most romantic and useful plant.

Quamoclit

Quamoclit lobata has synonyms of *Ipomoea lobata and Mina lobata* and is a rather surprising member of the Convolvulaceae family, nothing like the Hedge Bindweed which scrambles through British hedgerows. It is a splendid Mexican climber, very prolific in its flowering, which we grew as an annual with its finger-like flowers which open scarlet and change through orange to white, making it an ideal attention-grabber in the front garden to attract passers-by so that we had the privilege of many a visual cameo as they paused to admire such an exotic sight in the middle of Bedford.

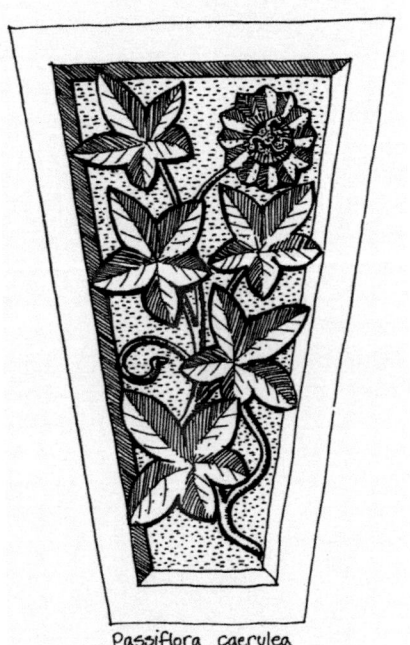

Passiflora caerulea
Albany Road - Bedford

We grew it to scramble, like its native cousins, through our own urban "fedge" consisting of several varieties of ivy which interwove to create an evergreen hedge over a low wrought iron fence. This was a good background on which to display a few more restrained annual and perennial climbers to keep company with the Quamoclit and to create a changing, colourful display over a long period. My collector's instinct for sweet peas knows no limits but *Lathyrus tingitanus* and *L.chlorantha* are not often seen but kept good company with *Eccremocarpus scaber* with its orange flowers and warted seed pods. Perhaps the most exotic partner in this riotous tangle was the *Passiflora caerulea*, the humble Passion Flower of my childhood which hung from star-apple trees where my cousins and I would risk life and limb over fast-flowing streams to climb up to pick their delicious fruit. Other residents of Bedford grew these round their doors whilst the keystones in the arches above were decorated with carved stonework depicting the same plant.

Rosa

Rosa gallica officinalis is one of the oldest varieties of rose, having been cultivated by the Greeks and Romans who used their petals to scent their baths, as decorations and for showering over brides at weddings, the origins of confetti. In the 10th century, Arab physicians distilled the essential oil from the flowers for use in medicines and perfumery. It was brought to Provins in France from the Valley of Damascus by Thibaut le Chansonnier on his return from the Crusades. In 13th century Provins, an industry began which flourished for six centuries and was based on the discovery that the petals from this rose retained their fragrance when dried and powdered, a characteristic we observed in our own specimens. The apothecaries developed conserves and confections which, over the period, they offered to Joan of Arc, Louis XIV and Napoleon amongst a host of French dignitaries, and the rose thus became known as the "Apothecary's Rose". It was also the Red Rose of Lancaster, adopted by Henry V as his royal emblem.

As a child, I was told by my father that there were rose gardens in India so large that you could get lost in them, so I valued my modest collection of roses every bit as highly as any medieval physician would have done. I dried thousands of blooms on the string platform of my Pakistani 'charpai', a real bed of roses, and used these both for their fragrance and their colour in my own home-made pot-pourri in dry and wet forms. I recreated Elizabethan recipes using my own Apothecary's Rose together with *Rosa chinensis, Madame Isaac Pereire, Constance Spry, Rose de Resht*, mixed with lavender, lemon verbena, orris root, cinnamon, cloves, various essential oils and more. Some people are uncomfortable picking flowers, but I picked them unashamedly, knowing as I do that all my plants will give more and prosper for my need. They are not like us because there is no limit to their giving. The Lebanese poet Khalil Gibran observed that "they give that they might live, for to withhold is to perish". We collected the fresh buds of all our roses to experiment with a 17th century recipe for incense cones which was a superbly-scented success, justifying the high regard placed on perfumes, in many forms, in both ancient and modern times. In a less dynamic form, we also made a paste of the ingredients and modelled this into aromatic beads with frankincense and myrrh, oil of clary, all bound with gum tragacanth. When worn next to the skin, the body temperature releases the fragrance about the person. And what more beautiful addition to a wholesome salad than fresh rose petals?

Solanum

Solanum laciniatum is the Poroporo of New Zealand and the Kangaroo Apple of Australia. It was a particular delight to find it had survived the winter beneath a young white mulberry tree in front of our west-facing garden wall. The gorgeous hanging bunches of blue flowers meeting my eyes at about five feet above ground level were a real treat, as indeed were the many glistening green berries which followed. But the fruits are poisonous when green, being full of alkaloids and steroids. The toxic principle is the glycoside solasonine which hydrolises to the alkaloid aglycone solasodine, and until 1981 it was grown commercially in New Zealand for the solasodine which is used as a base for steroid hormone synthesis.

When we grew plants like this in our garden, we had no idea of the complex nature of the chemistry we were about to unleash. However, the concentration of the solasodine reduces significantly in the orange ripe fruit which can then safely be used to make jam, like the early settlers of New Zealand, or even be eaten fresh. It was introduced to Britain in 1772, but in 1999 it enjoyed brief notoriety in the media who reported that the Northumberland village of East Cramlington was obliged to take out public liability insurance because of "unexpected hallucinogenic properties" of plants growing in a community garden! Knowledge of this kind certainly made us think twice about using the fruits, so we were content with the beauty of the plant.

It is sometimes confused with *Solanum aviculare*. Whilst they share some general features, they are quite distinctly different in others, not least that *S.aviculare* is twice the height at nearly 12 feet in the specimens which grew side by side in our garden.

Tropaeolum

Tropaeolum tuberosum is the tuberous nasturtium, a perennial climber distinguished by its spectacular red and orange, long-spurred flowers. Our modern cultivar, *Ken Aslet*, is worthy of the medieval aspirations of beauty and usefulness although it has no appreciable scent. We planted it on a tripod adjacent to the path so that we could encounter its entrancing little orange birds floating out of the foliage. Its reputation for being short-lived and behaving better as an annual could be due to the fact that every year it produces a nest of new tubers which sits above the ground, and if it is not covered or replanted, the plant would perish in a hard winter.

It is a South American climber native to Peru, Chile and Bolivia where it is known as "anu". In the Andes, the purple marbled tubers are boiled and sweetened before being eaten, but are considered a delicacy in Bolivia if they are frozen after boiling. We simply boiled them and served them buttered with a squeeze of lemon and black pepper. The taste was reminiscent of artichokes with a suggestion of turpentine fragrance which left us much preferring the artichokes. It was introduced to Europe in 1827 and is still cultivated in some parts as a vegetable.

I initially grew this plant for one purpose and ended up using it for many others. I first grew it for its leaves and flowers which are high in vitamin C. I also learned that its flower buds and seeds could be pickled like capers. But I also grew it under the apple tree as a companion plant where it deterred wooly aphids. Medicinally, the seeds yield an antibiotic, the leaves are antibacterial and, as I found on a postcard from Kew, the fibres from its stems can be used to make a delicate lace.

Umbellifers

Umbelliferae, the carrot family, is a large group of plants and, like most families, plant or human, encompasses all sorts of characters and personalities. There are rogues, thugs, beauties, rarities and those which are so useful in our lives that we just cannot contemplate life without them. Such is Coriander, *Coriandrum sativum*, a culinary plant from India where its roasted and ground seeds are the main ingredient of an authentic curry. But its popularity increases throughout the world, and there is hardly a cuisine anywhere that does not demand it in one form or another. It spread through Europe with the Romans who valued it both as a spice and a medicine, and who attempted to create a corner of home anywhere they had the chance to set up a garden, in the same way that to this day, it is a virtual obligation in the Italian community of Bedford to plant a grape vine and oregano.

The history of the uses of Coriander is impressive. In Ayurvedic medicine it is used to treat nosebleeds and vertigo, as a diuretic and to relieve fevers, conjunctivitis and as a stimulant. Its aromatic fresh green leaves are used as a herb, chopped for sprinkling over meats, vegetables, yoghurt dips and salads. It was one of the embalming herbs of the ancient Egyptians and seeds were found in Tutankhamun's tomb. Hippocrates and other Greek physicians are known to have used it medicinally, and it was a plant included in the earliest European medical herbaria. In England, long before the invention of refrigerators, its seeds were used with vinegar to preserve meat as pickling spices are still used today. A 16th century list of "Herbys necessary for a gardyn" includes coriander as a herb for pottage, a thick soup. It is, indeed, a time-traveller of the highest order.

Coriander is a quietly pretty plant in its own right, its flowers being delicate in appearance like those of its British native cousin, Queen Anne's Lace or, more prosaically, Cow Parsley, *Anthriscus sylvestris*. When I grew it amongst colourful annuals such as cornflowers, I created a very interesting show. But having struggled to keep herb beds under control, I eventually resorted to growing herbs in pots, either as single specimens or groups of more than one variety of those which are compatible. They could then be shown off to advantage, moved to the sunniest positions or kept right outside the kitchen door to be picked fresh to add flavour to stews and salads alike. And, of course, it is a lot easier to harvest the seeds when they are ripe without getting varieties mixed up.

Viola

Viola odorata is the sweet violet of Europe and Asia, held in such warm affection by everyone, and around which so many romantic legends have built up over centuries. The seeking out of its shy flowers on nature walks with our children or waiting for the first signs of spring in our own garden, was one of our greatest pleasures. The sweet, strong scent of its flowers has been used famously in perfumes, cosmetics, medicines, confectionery and wines. It was much cultivated for commercial purposes in Stratford-upon-Avon where the Bard made so many references to flowers in his plays, as Orsino, Duke of Illyria, comparing music to the food of love in "Twelfth Night", goes on to evoke "the sweet sound that breathes upon a bank of violets, stealing and giving odour!" in recognition that the perfume reaches another sense.

Nowadays violets are grown commercially in the south of France where the liqueur "Creme de Violette" is produced. The flowers are also candied and used in confectionery, and a decoction of the leaves can be used to treat coughs. The Emperor Napoleon was one of the most famous devotees of the humble violet because they reminded him of the Corsican woods in which he played as a child. He presented them often to Josephine, and gave them to her to wear on her wedding day and to mark the subsequent anniversaries. It was adopted as the emblem of the Imperial Napoleonic Party as the Emperor promised his followers that he would return from exile in Elba when the violets appeared in the spring. Violets which Napoleon had picked from Josephine's grave were found in a locket round his neck when he died.

Its reputation in folk medicine is as impressive as its romantic one. Its syrup was used for relieving whooping cough, sore throats, even tuberculosis and other diseases of the lungs. It was also recommended for headaches, migraine and insomnia, and research confirms that it contains the glycoside of salicylic acid used in the synthesis of aspirin. The roots also contain the alkaloid violine.

Withania

Withania somnifera is a rarely seen little treasure of a plant from the Mediterranean, Africa and India. It is a modest perennial shrub of the Solanaceae family which made a neat round plant for me and flowered and fruited well, but it behaved as an annual. The dainty yellow-orange fruits encased in an inflated calyx not unlike miniatures of its relatives the Chinese Lantern and the Cape Gooseberry, have earned it the common name of Winter Cherry. They are, in fact, poisonous and narcotic as they contain the alkaloid somniferin which has hypnotic properties.

Nevertheless, the plant has a long history of use. Ayurvedic physicians use only the roots and leaves for their drugs. They believe it to be an aphrodisiac as well as an effective tonic for relieving fevers and stress and general debility and memory lapses in the elderly. The powdered roots can be made into an invigorating tonic to restore the health of children emaciated by famine and it can also be used systematically against wasting diseases. Fruits threaded onto strips of date palm leaves have been found in ancient Egyptian burials and in garlands in Tutankhamun's tomb. I could appreciate this intrinsic quality of these small fruits as I incorporated them in some of my own garlands and wreaths along with the larger lanterns of *Physalis alkekengi variegata*.

Xeranthemum

Xeranthemum annuum is one of many species of everlasting flowers from the Compositae family and comes from the steppes and stony banks of Iran and the Caucasus. So beloved of flower arrangers, they were called "straw flowers" and "immortelles" by the Victorians who made much use of them in posies and intricate flower pictures which can still be seen in books and museums. Their popularity nowadays is abundantly evident in the variety of seeds available for a wide range of plants which I grew in my Bedford garden, not only for the dried flowers but also for the fascination of the grains which are used as cereals in the Andes, for making bread and tortillas in Ecuador. The arrangements that can be made from the flowers can be seen in garden centres, High Street shops and florists who make them to add colour and fragrance to dentists' waiting rooms.

Lunaria annua
Uniola sp.
Coix lacryma-jobi

I used these flowers in combination with other dried materials, grasses, pods and vine trails from a number of different climbers to construct swags, plaits, garlands and wreaths, setting the fine texture of grains from *Eragrostis abbesinica*, *Amaranthus hypochondriacus* and *Chenopodium quinoa* against the more robust seed pods of Henbane, Silkweed, Evening Primrose and the papery discs of *Lunaria annua*. Topiary trees constructed from green Oregano flowers with highlights of the yellow flowers of *Helichrysum setosa* and white flowers of *Amobium alatum,* set out in striking patterns on a cone of oasis foam, achieved a different scale from the extremely miniature baskets I painstakingly filled with the individual flowers of the same plants. The arrangements which could be made from this cornucopia of materials were endless, limited only by the imagination. I would never mind being immortal amongst them.

Yew

Taxus baccata is the English Yew of country churchyards and topiary hedging. Some specimens are estimated to be more than 2000 years old and the tree has innovative ways to regenerate, ensuring its longevity. It was favoured by the clergy as a substitute foliage for use in the church on Palm Sunday as palm leaves were not readily available. It was also considered safer to enclose the trees within the churchyard to prevent cattle from browsing on its poisonous leaves, although a decoction of these has been used in Switzerland to treat troublesome insects on livestock. The temptingly delicious-looking sticky red berries are also poisonous as they fall to make a red carpet on the pavement in St Peter's Square in Bedford. The birds notoriously ate them and dropped the seeds to leave seedlings all over our garden. We lifted these to grow on in pots, knowing that it would be a long time before we might see our own berries. However, they made delightful little potted pets and, if they are kept long enough and potted on, after ten years we found that one specimen made a most elegant substitute for a Christmas tree.

Modern medicine is increasing the value of this plant in cancer research, with drug companies soliciting clippings from the public. The wood is very desirable for use in furniture-making and is also made into walking sticks, knife handles, comb backs and carving. It is said to have been the favoured wood for the ancient longbows of medieval England. How would we have fared at Agincourt in 1415 but for the power of those?

Zantedeschia

Zantedeschia aethiopica is the Arum Lily of the Aroid family, a very architectural plant which deserves a prominent place in any garden in order to display its handsome leaves and puritanical white spathes, named after the Italian botanist and physicist F Zantedeschi. It comes from the damp flat swampy areas around Cape Town in South Africa rather than Ethiopia. In the 18th century the style "aethiopica" was applied to any part of the African continent of which little was known at that time. It has become naturalised in Australia but is becoming an agricultural weed. Its large rhizomes contain starch and have been used as food for domestic animals. The flowers are commonly used in funeral bouquets.

Its egg-shaped ovaries develop into berries in the same way as its British native cousin, the Cuckoo-pint, and both of these plants grew in the damp, shady area of our north-facing border, keeping good company with a standard honeysuckle, *Lonicera fragrantissima* and our *Nandina domestica*.

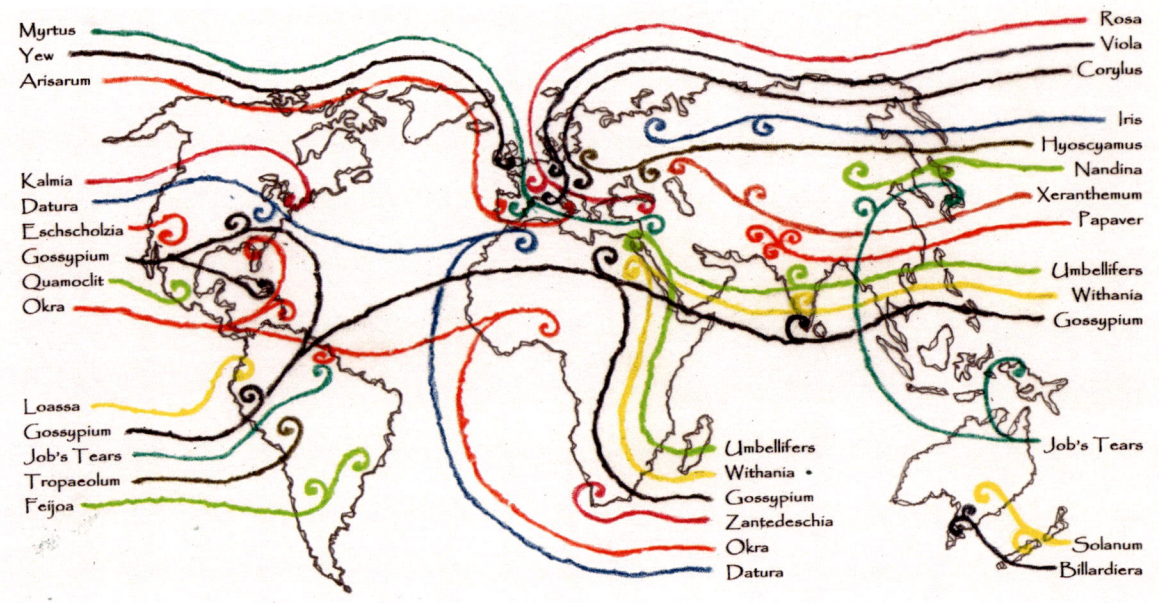

Myrtus
Yew
Arisarum

Rosa
Viola
Corylus

Iris
Hyoscyamus
Nandina
Xeranthemum
Papaver

Kalmia
Datura
Eschscholzia
Gossypium
Quamoclit
Okra

Umbellifers
Withania
Gossypium

Loassa
Gossypium
Job's Tears
Tropaeolum
Feijoa

Umbellifers
Withania
Gossypium
Zantedeschia
Okra
Datura

Job's Tears

Solanum
Billardiera

Old explorers' charts showed their routes across the known world, newly surveyed coastlines and conjectured parts to inspire others to complete their mission. We felt like those explorers as we gathered our information of plants which had travelled from place to place, often with those same explorers, and for many other reasons beyond their natural distribution by birds, animals, insects and the elements. The plants have been hunted by botanists in the name of science, in the cause of commerce, in the barbarous trading of slaves, or just to satisfy the whims of dilettante collectors. They have carried with them the mysteries of their uses as food, as medicines, as cosmetics, as perfumes and as narcotics. They have provided the raw materials for the manufacture of tools, weapons, paper, fabrics, baskets, dyes, paints and much more to enhance the basic qualities of life. They have brought comfort in times of grief, confidence in the initiation into tribes, ceremony in death, and even death itself.

All of their history, geography, sociology, anthropology and mythology has come together in a small garden, transforming it into a veritable time machine, bringing purpose, interest and magic to the noble practice of gardening.